A Kid's Guide to Drawing™
How to Draw
Animals
of the
Rain Forest

Justin Lee

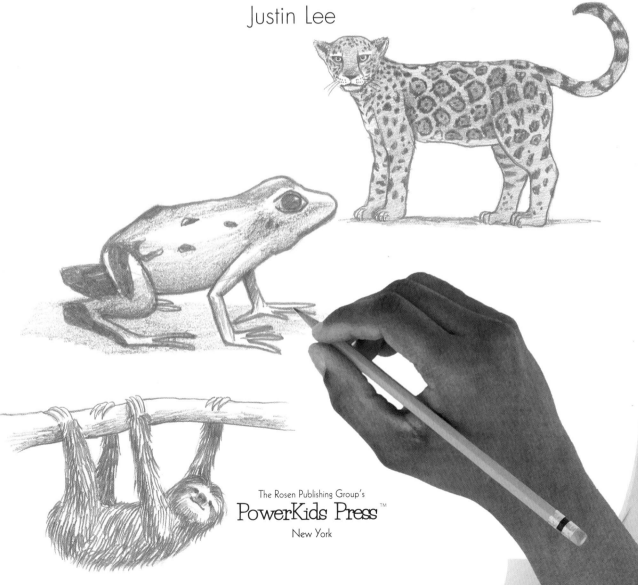

The Rosen Publishing Group's
PowerKids Press™
New York

For Heidi, my sister and one of my best friends

Published in 2002 by The Rosen Publishing Group, Inc.
29 East 21st Street, New York, NY 10010

First Edition

Book Design: Kim Sonsky

Layout: Michael Caroleo

Project Editor: Frances E. Ruffin

Photo Credits: p.6 © Staffan Widstrand/CORBIS; pp. 8, 20 © Tom Brakefield/CORBIS; p. 10 © Buddy Mays/CORBIS; p. 12 © Kevin Schafer/CORBIS; p. 14 © Joe MacDonald/CORBIS; p. 16 © David A. Northcott/CORBIS; p. 18 © The Purcell Team/CORBIS.

Lee, Justin, 1973–
How to draw animals of the rain forest / Justin Lee.—1st ed.
    p. cm. — (A kid's guide to drawing) Includes index.
ISBN 0-8239-5793-4 (lib. bdg.)
1. Rain forest animals in art—Juvenile literature. 2. Drawing—Technique—Juvenile literature. [1. Rain forest animals in art. 2. Drawing—Technique. 3. Animals in art.] I. Title. II. Series
NC783.8.F67 L44 2002
743.6—dc21   00-012442

CONTENTS

Let's Draw Rain Forest Animals

When we think of **tropical rain forests,** we can almost smell the dark soil and the warm, humid air found there. How much do we actually know about the world's rain forests and the animals who live in them? Tropical rain forests are found on either side of the **equator**. There are no changing seasons in tropical rain forests. The temperatures are warm, sometimes hot, all year. Most rain forests get at least 70 inches (180 cm) of rain per year. Tropical rain forests are found in three areas of the world. Southeast Asia, Indonesia, and parts of Australia are rain forest areas. West and Central Africa are other rain forest areas. A large area of rain forest stretches from Central America to South America. Sixty million years ago, tropical rain forests covered almost all of Earth. Tropical rain forests now cover only a small percent of the world's land.

Unfortunately, our rain forests are disappearing. By learning to draw rain forest animals, not only will you sharpen your artistic skills but you also will learn about this valuable part of our world.

Here is a list of supplies that you will need to draw rain forest animals:

- A sketch pad
- A number 2 pencil
- A pencil sharpener
- An eraser

All of the drawings begin with a few simple shapes. The basic shapes you will use are ovals, circles, curved lines, rectangles, and triangles. To learn more about these terms, turn to page 22. Some drawings call for crosshatching. To crosshatch, draw a series of parallel lines that run into each other.

Our rain forests took millions and millions of years to become what they are today. The animals that live there are very different from each other. Some are fast and some are slow. The same is true of people. Everyone learns to draw at different speeds. If it takes you a little longer to draw the pictures in this book, don't worry. Keep trying and pretty soon your pictures will be as wonderful as the animals that live in our rain forests.

Toucan

Brightly colored toucans live high in the branches of South and Central American rain forests. Their noisy call rings out as they fly from tree to tree. They usually travel in pairs or small groups. There are about 40 different **species** of toucans. Some are as small as 7 inches (18 cm). Others grow to be as big as 25 inches (64 cm). Toucans have large, colorful beaks, which can be half as long as their bodies. Although a toucan's beak is extremely large, it is also light. Toucans are called soft-beaked birds because they eat soft food, such as fruit. When a toucan eats, it grabs a piece of fruit with the end of its beak and then tilts back its head and lets the fruit run into its mouth. Occasionally toucans eat small lizards and insects.

1

Draw a horizontal branch. Above it, at an angle, draw a tilted oval, not quite touching the branch. Add vertical lines for the legs, with claws wrapping around the branch.

2

Add the wing, with a slight bulge at the shoulder. Draw lines on the wing to suggest feathers.

3

Extend the bottom of the oval for the tail. Draw the end of the tail behind and below the branch, with lines for feathers. Add small, curved lines on the claws. Shade the leg.

4

Draw a line from the shoulder for the top of the head. Make the front of the head vertical where the beak attaches. Draw the throat. Add the eye, and the triangle around it. Outline the white area on the front of the body.

5

Now draw the beak. First look carefully at its curves. Make the top part of the beak wider than the bottom. Add the dark spot at the tip. Draw the tongue.

6

Look at the final drawing. Shade the dark areas of the bird. Add the pattern to the beak. Darken lines that seem important. Add shading to the branch.

Howler Monkey

The howler monkey has a voice box that is ten times as big as a human's. Its loud screams can be heard up to 3 miles (5 km) away. The howler monkey uses its voice almost like a weapon. Instead of fighting, often two male howler monkeys will scream at one another. Screaming also lets other groups of monkeys in the area know that the howlers are there and they are using that space.

Howler monkeys live in the rain forests of South and Central America. Full-grown howler monkeys can weigh more than 15 pounds (6.8 kg) and can be 2 feet (61 cm) long, not counting their tails. Their strong tails can be just as long as their bodies. The howlers use their tails to grab onto branches and hang from trees while eating.

1

Start by drawing three overlapping ovals. Notice how each tilts at a different angle.

2

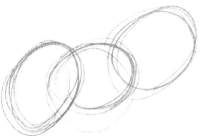

Draw the face, one feature at a time, starting with the mouth.

3

Add the outline of the head, and join the ovals to make the curved back. Draw the arm and leg on the side closest to you. Pay attention to the way they bend. Add fur to the chin.

4

Draw the remaining arm and leg, and the tail. As you draw them, add branches. Notice how the tail curls around one branch.

5

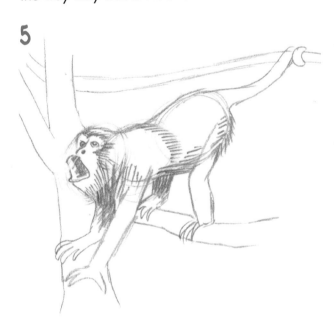

Use your eraser to clean up lines you won't need in the finished drawing. Starting with the darkest areas, make short pencil lines for fur.

6

Look carefully at which parts of the monkey are darkest, and which are lightest. Continue adding fur. Draw shading on the branches.

Sloth

The sloth is one of the slowest animals in the world. The word slothful means lazy. Actually, the sloth isn't lazy. It has a very slow **metabolism**. The sloth's body moves very slowly and it uses very little energy. It sleeps an average of 15 hours per day! Three-toed sloths live in the rain forests of South America, from Brazil to southern Argentina. They can grow to be 2 feet (61 cm) long and can weigh as much as 9.5 pounds (4.3 kg). They are covered in brownish or grayish hair. During the rainy season, **algae** grows all over the sloth's hair, making the animal look green.

The sloth spends its days hanging upside down from the branches of trees. It moves slowly through the branches, eating leaves.

1

Draw two lines for the tree branch. Make it interesting by adding curves. Below the branch, draw an oval for the sloth's body.

2

Draw straight lines upward for the legs, at angles. Notice how one leg overlaps part of the one behind it. Draw just part of one front leg, to save space for the head.

3

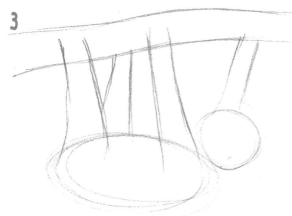

Lightly draw a circle for the head. Where is it in relation to the body?

4

Add claws curving around the branch. Begin to add fur with short, downward strokes. The fur on a sloth grows this way because the sloth spends most of its life upside down!

5

Draw the face by starting with a small line for the mouth, at an angle, in the center of the circle. Add the nose, and the eyes just to the side of the nose. Draw dark fur areas extending from the eyes. Add short pencil strokes for the fur on the arms and legs, and on the back and neck.

6

Keep drawing short pencil lines to add fur to the rest of the body. Notice the areas that are darker, and the direction of the lines. Shade the tree branch. Fix any details you might have missed. Finally, clean up any smudges with your eraser.

Poison Dart Frog

There are about 170 species of dart frogs that are poisonous. They live high in the trees of the Central and South American rain forests. They call to each other in shrill chirps and trills. They feed on the many insects that live in the forest. Poison dart frogs are tiny, usually no more than 1 or 2 inches (2.5–5 cm) long. The male frogs defend their territory by wrestling with other frogs. Other frogs blend into their environment so they won't be seen and eaten. Poison dart frogs are very brightly colored and patterned. Their bright colors warn other animals to stay away.

People use these frogs for their poison. The Choco Indians of the rain forest dip their arrows in the poison on the frogs' backs. Some of the poisons are so strong that a small amount will kill a person.

1

Draw two overlapping ovals. Draw them very lightly! You'll see why in a moment.

2

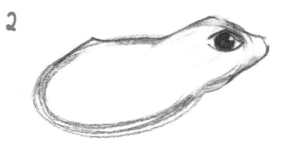

Add a bump for the hip, a bump at the top of the head, a bump for the nose, and one more for the throat. Erase the ovals where they overlap. Draw a circle for the eye, and leave a small, white spot when you darken it. Add the curving lines for the top and bottom of the eye.

3

Add the legs. Look at where and how each leg attaches to the body, and at the angles of each segment of the legs. Erase the oval where the leg overlaps it.

4

Add shading as your pencil gets dull. Leave part of the back very light to make it look shiny. When you sharpen your pencil, go over details and outlines to make them sharper. Add the cast shadow under the frog. Clean up any smudges with your eraser.

Emerald Tree Boa

The emerald tree boa spends its entire life high in the dense branches of the South American rain forest **canopy**. This snake almost never is found on the forest floor. The emerald tree boa can grow to be over 6 feet (183 cm) long. It spends its days hanging motionless in a loose coil from a branch. The snake's green skin blends with the leaves of the tree. The white markings make it difficult for **predators** to see it.

At night, the snake hunts for food by hanging from a branch. Boas have special **organs** in their mouths called Jacobson's organs. They allow the boa to "smell" the air. As soon as the snake detects a passing animal, usually a small mammal, bird, or lizard, it lunges forward and gets its next meal.

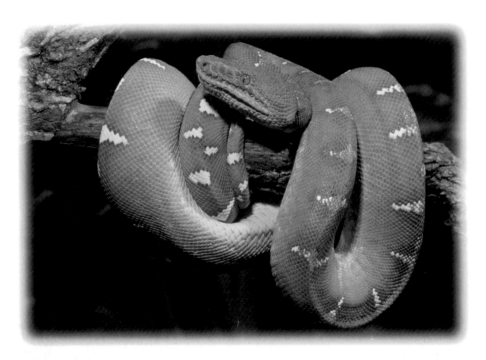

1

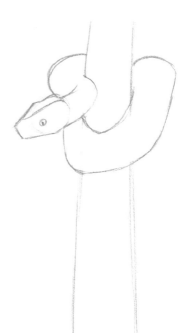

Start with two light, vertical lines for the vine. Draw the head and eye, and the first section of the body, overlapping part of the vine. Make the front of the head blunt. Each eyebrow bulges slightly.

2

Add the next section of the body, forming a rough U shape.

3

Below the U shape, make another section of the body, this time a fat C shape. Add two more sections, getting smaller and smaller. Notice that the snake doesn't wrap around the vine in one continuous spiral. The tail wraps all the way around, but the larger parts of the body reverse direction to form 'clamps' to hold to the vine.

Now try to make the snake and vine look round. Look carefully for the pattern of curving, white spots. Crosshatch to suggest scales, shade on the snake and the vine, and cast shadows on the vine and snake.

15

Green Iguana

The green iguana lives in the branches of the South American rain forest. This lizard can grow to over 5 feet (152 cm) in length. It has a line of spiny scales, like little horns, running down its back. Its whole body usually is covered with bright green scales, but sometimes they can be blue or brown or even red. Iguanas also have sharp teeth and claws that they use to defend themselves. Iguanas may look scary, but they aren't very dangerous to humans. They would rather hide than fight. In fact, when they are threatened they drop from tree branches into a pond or river and swim away.

Iguanas are active during the day. They **forage** in the forest for green, leafy plants to eat. They also spend a lot of time lying in the sun.

1

Begin with the swooping shape for the body. Notice how the bottom line becomes almost vertical at the head. Don't join the lines at the tail yet. It gets a lot longer!

2

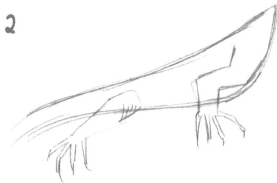

Look at the legs. The front leg starts at the shoulder, goes down, back, then down again. The back leg is foreshortened. This means that part of it (the part connecting to the body) comes straight toward you. Now draw the legs, and add toes and claws.

3

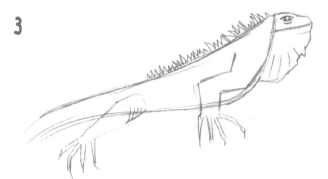

Add the top of the head, and the eye. Draw a line for the mouth, then add the flaps of skin beneath the mouth. Add the distinct, jagged row of spikes along the iguana's back. They don't need to be even.

4

Looking closely at the example (or at a photo, or better yet, a real iguana if you have one handy!), add the tail and details. Crosshatching suggests scales on the legs and head. Around the mouth, add shapes you see in the example. Add a branch under the iguana. To make it more interesting, add a vine or two spiraling around it.

5

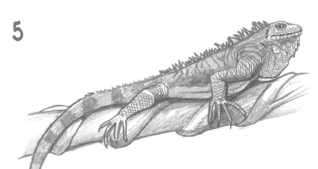

Now take your time as you turn your sketch into a finished drawing. Work slowly and carefully, paying close attention to details. Look at shading. Make the shading darkest where the branch is close to the iguana's body. Add the stripes on the tail. After shading, darken lines with a sharp pencil. Clean up any smudges with your eraser. Admire your creation!

Gorilla

   Gorillas are one of humankind's closest relatives. They can live up to 50 years. They nurse their young and live in family units. Some scientists have taught gorillas to communicate with humans. Gorillas travel through the thick rain forests of Central and West Africa. They live in family groups of 5 to 30 individuals. Each group has one **dominant** male, called a silverback. When a male gorilla becomes **mature**, the black hair on his back turns a grayish, silver color. The male silverback is responsible for protecting the female gorillas and the children in his family. A full-grown silverback can be 5 feet and 6 inches (168 cm) tall and can weigh as much as 310 pounds (141 kg). Adult females only grow to about half the size of the male.

1

Draw two small circles on top of a larger oval. Make a line across them to emphasize the strong brow of the gorilla.

2

Draw a line for the mouth. Add eyes, with lines under them. Draw slanting nostrils.

3

From the edge of the eyebrow, draw a line up to a point and back down—like a pyramid on the gorilla's head. This part of the head is almost as high as the face! Draw the ear and short pencil lines on the chin, cheeks, and forehead.

4

From the back of the head, make a long swooping line for the back, joined by another swooping line for the back of the leg.

5

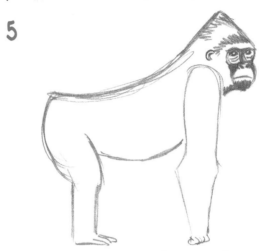

Lightly draw the leg and arm, with toes and fingers. Notice the shape of the arm. Look how close the shoulder comes to the face.

6

Add the other leg and arm. Before you add fur, make light guidelines to remind you in which direction the shading needs to go.

7

Cover the whole body with short pencil strokes. Be sure to follow the direction of your guidelines. Pay attention to areas that are lighter and darker. Go over lines that need to be darker or sharper, and refine details of the face if you need to. Add a cast shadow underneath.

19

Jaguar

Jaguars are the biggest cats in the Americas. A full-grown male jaguar can be almost 6 feet long (183 cm) and can weigh as much as 265 pounds (120 kg). At one time, the jaguar lived as far north as Colorado, but now it no longer lives in the United States, and only a few live in Mexico. The jaguar lives mostly between southern Mexico and northern Argentina. Many jaguars live in the tropical rain forests. Jaguars live near water where they can stay cool on hot days.

Jaguars are predators and will eat almost any animal. Some of their favorite foods are deer, sloths, monkeys, small animals, and fish. When a jaguar sees its **prey**, it stalks it quietly. Jaguars are so fierce that they have no natural enemies.

1

Start by drawing two light, overlapping circles.

2

Add the two sides of the mouth slanting downward, with the small vertical line in the center.

3

Add a flat triangle for the nose.

4

Directly above the outside of the nose, draw two upside-down L shapes.

5

Make eyes by drawing curves down from the outside of the L shapes. Add ears.

6

Make circles for the centers of the eyes—leave small highlights in them.

7

Darken the rest of each eye. Add rows of dots on the muzzle. Add whiskers.

8

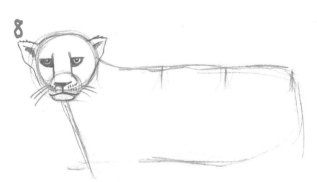

Measure three heads back for the length of the body. Make the back level with the bottom of the eyes, with a little curve at the neck. Make the front of the body slant slightly.

9

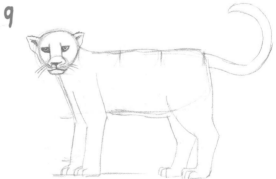

Add the legs and paws. Draw lightly at first. Look at your jaguar. Is everything the way you want it? If something looks wrong, try looking at your picture in a mirror, or hold it up to a light and look through the back.

10

Next add spots to the jaguar—dark patches, with one or more darker spots inside. These large spots become smaller spots and stripes on the legs and tail. Lightly lay out the pattern, then carefully add shading. It takes awhile, but it's worth it!

Drawing Terms

Here are some of the words and shapes you will need to draw animals of the rain forest:

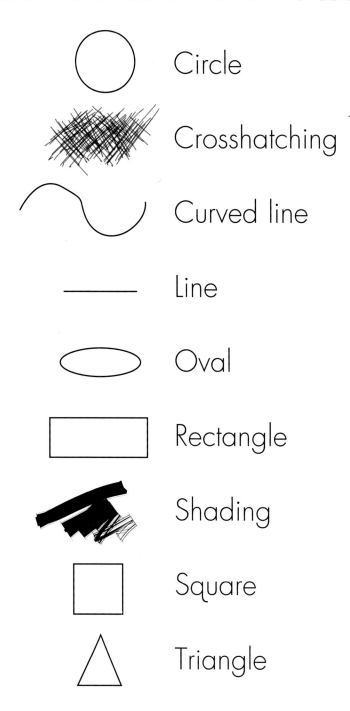

Circle

Crosshatching

Curved line

Line

Oval

Rectangle

Shading

Square

Triangle

Glossary

algae (AL-jee) Tiny plants without roots or stems that usually live in water.

canopy (KA-nuh-pee) The high roof of the rain forest made by all the leaves and branches of the trees.

dominant (DAH-mih-nent) In charge.

equator (ih-KWAY-tur) An imaginary line around Earth that separates it into two parts, north and south.

forage (FOR-ij) To hunt or search for something.

mature (muh-TOOR) Adult.

metabolism (meh-TA-buh-lih-zum) The speed at which the body processes energy.

organs (OR-genz) Parts of a plant or an animal.

predators (PREH-duh-terz) Animals that kill other animals for food.

prey (PREY) Animals that are hunted by other animals for food.

rain forests (RAYN FOR-ests) Very wet areas that have many kinds of plants, trees, and animals.

species (SPEE-sheez) A single kind of plant or animal. For example, people are one species.

tropical (TRAH-pih-kul) An area that is hot and humid.

Index

Web Sites

To learn more about rain forest animals, check out these Web sites:
www.animalsoftherainforest.org
www.ran.org/kids_action/index1.html